# The Best 50

# BAKED POTATO
# RECIPES

### Christie Katona

BRISTOL PUBLISHING ENTERPRISES
Hayward, California

©2007 Bristol Publishing Enterprises
2714 McCone Ave., Hayward, California 94545.
World rights reserved. No part of this publication
may be reproduced in any form, nor may it be stored in a retrieval
system, transmitted, or otherwise copied for public or private use
without prior written permission from the publisher.

Printed in the United States of America.

ISBN-13: 978-1-55867-337-3
ISBN-10: 1-55867-337-7

Cover design:          Frank J. Paredes
Cover photography:     John A. Benson
Recipe consultant:     Randy Mon

# ALL ABOUT POTATOES

Nutritionists have shown that potatoes are low in calories, are an excellent source of complex carbohydrates, are high in vitamins and fiber, and contain no fat or cholesterol. An average baked potato (sans toppings) has about 110 calories or about the same number of calories as a large apple or $\frac{1}{2}$ cup of cottage cheese.

I view the potato as a wholesome base—like rice—to which you can add an endless variety of delicious toppings and sauces that can be either rich or as healthy and diet-conscious as you like. I have included a wide variety of recipes to suit almost every palate. I have included low-calorie dishes, vegetarian dishes, and delicious dishes that use sweet potatoes and yams. There is also a section on fast family meals for busy parents.

In addition to the recipes, included is some interesting background information on potatoes and basic information you should have for buying, storing, preparing, and serving your potato dishes.

## SOUTH AMERICAN ORIGINS

The potato originated in the Peruvian Andes of South America and was one of the major staples in the diet of the Incas. Spanish explorers were the first to discover potatoes in the Andean village of Sorocota in 1537 and subsequently introduced them to Spain, where they were cultivated as a food crop. From Spain, cultivation of potatoes spread slowly to continental Europe and then to England; however, England did not cultivate them as a crop until the mid-18th century.

Since the potato grows well in cool, moist areas, it flourished in England and Ireland and became a major food staple in those countries. Many people remember the Irish Potato Famine from their history lessons. When the potato crops failed between 1845 and 1847 due to a blight, nearly one million people starved to death in Ireland and about the same number emigrated to escape the famine.

The first potatoes in the United States arrived at Jamestown, Virginia in 1621. Today, potatoes are grown in many states, with the top five potato-producing states being Idaho, Washington, North Dakota, Colorado and Wisconsin, in that order.

Potatoes are the fourth largest commercial crop in the world.

## POTATO VARIETIES

Potatoes are either thin-skinned, which are best suited for boiling, or thick-skinned, which are best suited for baking and frying. The most common thick-skinned variety is the Russet Burbank, named after Luther Burbank. It is also commonly known as the "Idaho potato," although it is also grown in Washington, Oregon and other potato-producing states.

## NUTRITION

A potato has about the same calories as a large apple and is high in nutritional value. Potatoes are an excellent source of complex carbohydrates. They are high in vitamins, high in fiber, and contain no fat or cholesterol. The complex carbohydrates are digested more slowly than simple carbohydrates like sugar, so they provide a sustained and steady amount of energy over a longer period of time: you can go longer between meals without feeling hungry.

The following tables provide the nutritional rating for 1 medium U.S. potato (150 grams or 5.33 oz.). However, these can vary depending on the potato type and where it is grown.

## U.S. RECOMMENDED DAILY ALLOWANCE

| | | | |
|---|---|---|---|
| Protein | 6% | Folic Acid | 8% |
| Vitamin A | * | Phosphorus | 8% |
| Vitamin C | 50% | Magnesium | 8% |
| Thiamin (B1) | 8% | Zinc | 2% |
| Riboflavin (B2) | 2% | Copper | 8% |
| Niacin | 10% | Pantothenic Acid | 4% |
| Calcium | * | *Contains less than 2% of the | |
| Iron | 6% | USRDA for this nutrient. | |
| Vitamin B6 | 15% | | |

## NUTRIENT

| | | | |
|---|---|---|---|
| Protein | 3 g | Potassium | 750 mg |
| Carbohydrate | 23 g | Dietary Fiber | 2.7 g |
| Fat | 0 g | Calories | 110 |
| Sodium | 10 mg | Cholesterol | 0 mg |

Most of the minerals in a potato are found in the cambium, which is the narrow layer just below the outer skin, whereas the other nutritional elements are found throughout the potato. So if you want your minerals, eat those skins!

## HOW TO SELECT AND STORE POTATOES

In general, potatoes with fewer eyes and that have shallow eyes are higher in quality. Avoid potatoes that are cracked, have sprouts, are wrinkled, or have a green appearance or soft dark areas.

Store potatoes in a cool, dark, well-ventilated area. The ideal storage temperature is between 45° and 48°. Do not store potatoes in the refrigerator. Also, avoid storing in plastic bags.

# COOKING AND SERVING POTATOES

Baking time depends on the size. As a rough guide, bake at 425° for 40 minutes for small potatoes, 50 minutes for medium size potatoes, and 60 minutes for large potatoes. If you want to be sure, use a thermometer. The potatoes are done when the internal temperature reads between 210° and 220° on the thermometer.

Convection oven: Preparation for convection cooking is identical to that for the conventional oven except that the cooking time and/or temperature is lowered, since the forced air circulation transfers the heat to the potatoes more quickly than the conventional oven. When placing the potatoes on the racks, make sure there is sufficient clearance between the potatoes for air circulation. As a guide, cook at 375° for 30 to 45 minutes, depending on size. Again, if you want to be sure, use an instant-reading thermometer to check for doneness.

Electric potato baker: These appliances allow you to bake 2 potatoes in about 25 minutes. Two metal skewers inserted into the potatoes speed cooking time, and the device uses only $\frac{1}{8}$ the power of a conventional oven.

## BLOSSOMING POTATOES

For the majority of the recipes in this book, you will be using baked russet potatoes. The best method for serving them attractively is a method called "blossoming." Using a fork, pierce the skin in the shape of a cross in the middle of the potato. Then, press the ends towards the center, which causes the meat of the potato to blossom upward. Alternately, you can split the potato horizontally down its length, and then use the fork to manually fluff the potato meat. For the best appearance, avoid cutting with a knife since this tends to flatten the surface.

Use the temperatures given for baking but test for doneness about two-thirds of the way through the allotted time. Increase or decrease the time as necessary.

# CLASSIC WHITE SAUCE

*Use a heavy-bottomed pan, and stir with either a wooden spoon or whisk. The butter and flour mixture is the thickening agent, called a "roux." Heating liquid before adding it to roux helps sauce go together more evenly. Stir in one direction only and stir constantly!*

¼ cup butter
¼ cup flour

2 cups warm milk
salt and white pepper to taste

In a heavy-bottomed saucepan over medium heat, melt butter. Sprinkle with flour and stir constantly so roux bubbles but does not brown. Gradually add warm milk to mixture, stirring constantly until a smooth sauce forms. Season to taste.

## VARIATIONS

Veloute Sauce: Use chicken stock instead of milk.

Supreme Sauce: Use chicken stock instead of milk. Beat 2 egg yolks with 2 tbs. heavy cream and blend into sauce without boiling.

Mornay Sauce: Stir 1 cup shredded cheese into *Classic White Sauce.*

# DEMI GLACE

*This is one of the classic French sauces, and is easy to freeze.*

| | |
|---|---|
| 3 tbs. oil | few mushroom peelings |
| 1 carrot | 1 tsp. tomato puree |
| 1 small onion | 1 bouquet garni (1 bay leaf, 1 |
| 1 stalk celery | sprig thyme, 2 parsley stalks |
| 3 tbs. flour | in a spice bag or cheesecloth) |
| 2 cups beef, veal or chicken stock | salt and pepper to taste |

Finely chop carrot, onion and celery. Heat oil in a shallow saucepan and add vegetables. Cook over low heat until barely colored and softened. Stir in flour and continue to cook slowly, stirring with a spoon until a good russet brown. Draw vegetables aside in pan and add 1½ cups of stock and remaining ingredients. Bring to a boil and half cover with a lid. Simmer for 25 minutes. At this point, add reserved ½ cup of cold stock and tip pan so fat can be skimmed off. Strain sauce through a sieve. Taste and season lightly.

# PARMESAN SAUCE

*For a quick vegetarian topping, steam or microwave vegetables of your choice and spoon into a baked potato. Top with this wonderful sauce. It's particularly good with broccoli, carrots and cauliflower.*

$1/2$ cup mayonnaise
$1/2$ cup whipping cream
$1/2$ cup sour cream
$1/4$ cup grated Parmesan cheese
2 tsp. fresh lemon juice

Combine all ingredients in a saucepan and whisk over low heat until smooth and cheese is melted. Be careful not to boil.

# MEXICAN CALIENTE CHEESE SAUCE

Serves: 4

*Arrange bowls of halved cherry tomatoes, sliced ripe olives, avocado cubes, sliced green onions and salsa in the center of the table so each person can top his potato as he wishes.*

1 lb. Monterey Jack cheese, shredded
½ lb. sharp cheddar, shredded
¼ cup flour
1 can (12 oz.) beer
1 clove garlic, minced

1 can (4 oz.) chopped green chiles
3 tsp. chili powder
cayenne to taste
4 potatoes, baked and blossomed

Shred cheeses and toss in a large bowl with flour. In a large saucepan, heat beer over medium high heat. Add garlic, slowly stir in cheese by the handful, and using a wooden spoon stir constantly in one direction only. When all the cheese has been added, stir in green chiles, chili powder and cayenne to taste. Divide hot cheese sauce evenly over prepared potatoes.

# SLOPPY JOE SPUDS

*Kids love these!*

1 lb. ground chuck
1 cup chopped onion
2 cloves garlic, minced
1 green bell pepper, chopped
1 can (15 oz.) tomato sauce
1/2 cup water
1 tsp. dried thyme

1/4 cup ketchup
1 tbs. cider vinegar
1 tsp. Worcestershire sauce
1/4 tsp. Tabasco Sauce
salt and pepper to taste
4 potatoes, baked and blossomed

In a large skillet over medium high heat, cook meat, onion, garlic and green pepper until meat is browned and vegetables are soft. Drain off any excess fat. Add remaining ingredients and simmer for 10 minutes. Taste and correct seasoning. Divide evenly over prepared potatoes.

# POPEYE'S FAVORITE

*For a version that's lower in calories, omit cheese sauce. Residual heat from the other ingredients is enough to cook the spinach.*

1 tbs. oil
1 clove garlic, minced
2 cups diced ham
2 tomatoes, seeded and
    chopped

½ small bunch spinach
2 cups *Mexican Caliente Cheese Sauce*, page 11
4 potatoes, baked and blossomed
¼ cup grated Parmesan cheese

In a skillet over medium high heat, sauté garlic in oil until soft. Add ham and tomatoes and cook through. Prepare spinach. Remove any large stems and discard. Wash spinach well and shake dry. Stack leaves and roll in a paper towel to blot excess moisture. Slice into ¼-inch slices crosswise. Add spinach to pan and cook briefly until just wilted. Add cheese sauce and heat ingredients together. Taste and adjust seasoning. Divide evenly over prepared potatoes. Sprinkle with Parmesan.

# CONFETTI EGGS AND HAM

Serves: 4

*Add a fresh fruit salad and pastry to complete your menu.*

2 tbs. oil
1/2 cup chopped onion
1/2 cup chopped green bell
  pepper
1/4 cup sliced fresh mushrooms
2 tbs. chopped fresh parsley
1 cup diced cooked ham
1 1/2 tsp. salt

1/2 tsp. pepper
1 tsp. Worcestershire sauce
2 tomatoes, seeded and chopped
2 tbs. butter
4 eggs
4 potatoes, baked and blossomed
2 tbs. grated Parmesan cheese
salt and pepper for seasoning

Heat oil in a large skillet. Over medium high heat, sauté onion until soft. Add bell pepper, mushrooms, parsley, ham and seasonings. Cook until pepper is tender-crisp. Add tomatoes to heat through. In a separate pan, heat butter and softly scramble eggs. Divide eggs evenly on top of prepared potatoes. Top with vegetable mixture and sprinkle with Parmesan. Season with salt and pepper.

## BAKED PORK WITH
## OLD-FASHIONED BBQ SAUCE

Serves: 4

*This is one of those cozy winter dinners that everyone loves.*

1 lb. boneless pork shoulder
2 tbs. salad oil
1 onion, chopped
½ cup chopped celery
2 tbs. cider vinegar
2 tbs. brown sugar
1 cup ketchup

3 tbs. Worcestershire sauce
½ tsp. dry mustard
½ cup water
¼ tsp. salt
¼ tsp. pepper
4 potatoes, baked and blossomed

Cut pork into 1-inch cubes and trim off any fat. In a heavy oven-proof skillet over medium high heat, cook pork cubes in oil until evenly browned. In a food processor or blender, combine remaining ingredients for sauce. Pour off any excess fat in skillet. Add sauce to skillet and stir well. Bake mixture in a 325° oven for 1 hour or until pork is very tender. Divide evenly over prepared potatoes.

# POTATOES BURGUNDY

*Try one of the exotic mushroom varieties: shiitake, chanterelle, enoki, or oyster mushrooms, instead of regular mushrooms.*

1/4 cup butter, divided
1 lb. top round steak, thinly
   sliced
salt and pepper to taste
2 medium onions, thinly sliced

1 lb. mushrooms, sliced
1/2 cup burgundy
4 potatoes, baked and blossomed
1 cup shredded Swiss cheese

Melt 2 tbs. of butter in a heavy skillet over high heat. Quickly stir-fry meat until done to your liking. Sprinkle with salt and pepper, remove from pan with a slotted spoon and set aside. Add 1 tbs. butter to pan drippings and sauté onions until golden. Remove and set aside. Add remaining butter to pan and cook mushrooms until tender. Add wine and heat through. Return onion and meat to pan. Divide mixture evenly over prepared potatoes. Top with cheese and set under broiler until cheese melts.

# STROGANOFF SPUDS

*Parsley adds flavor and just the right bit of color to many dishes.*

| | |
|---|---|
| 1 lb. top sirloin | 1 cup *Demi-Glace*, page 9 |
| 2 tbs. butter | 2 tbs. ketchup or tomato paste |
| 2 tbs. oil | salt and pepper to taste |
| 1 onion, cut into slivers | 1 cup sour cream |
| 1 clove garlic, minced | 4 potatoes, baked and blossomed |
| 8 oz. fresh mushrooms, quartered | 1 tbs. finely minced parsley |

Partially freeze meat. Cut into ¼-inch strips using a sharp knife. Heat butter and oil in a large skillet over medium high heat. Cook meat in 2 batches until browned and tender. Remove and set aside. Add onion to pan with garlic and cook until tender. Add mushrooms and cook until light brown. Return meat to pan. Add *Demi-Glace*, ketchup, salt and pepper. Cook to heat through. Stir in sour cream, but do not boil. Divide evenly over prepared potatoes and sprinkle with parsley.

# LAMB GRAVY

*For those who like lamb, this is real comfort food. Fix it for dinner some cold, rainy evening when you've had a rough day.*

1 lb. ground lamb
2 tbs. butter
1 clove garlic, minced
1 small onion, chopped
salt and pepper to taste
$\frac{1}{2}$ tsp. rosemary
2 cups brown gravy
4 potatoes, baked and blossomed

In a skillet over medium high heat, brown lamb until no longer pink. Drain and set aside. Heat butter and sauté garlic and onion until soft. Return lamb to skillet and season with salt, pepper and rosemary. Stir in gravy and heat through. Divide evenly over prepared potatoes.

# JOE'S SPECIAL

*Practically everyone has had this popular dish using eggs. For a change try it as a topping on a baked potato.*

1 lb. lean ground beef
2 tbs. oil
1 medium onion, chopped
2 cloves garlic, minced
1 cup sliced mushrooms
1 pkg. (10 oz.) frozen chopped
   spinach, thawed

1/4 tsp. nutmeg
1/4 tsp. oregano
salt and pepper to taste
4 potatoes, baked and blossomed
1/2 cup grated Parmesan cheese

In a large skillet, brown beef in oil over medium high heat. Add onion and garlic and cook until tender. Stir in mushrooms and cook until soft. Place spinach in a dishtowel and wring tightly to remove liquid. Add to skillet and heat through. Season to taste. Divide evenly over prepared potatoes and sprinkle with Parmesan.

# VEAL PARMIGIANA

Serves: 4

*Strips of chicken breast also work well in this recipe. There are now many excellent spaghetti sauces available at the grocery store.*

2 tbs. olive oil
8 oz. veal, cut in thin strips
1 green bell pepper, cored and coarsely chopped
8 oz. mushrooms, sliced
1 clove garlic, minced

salt and black pepper to taste
2 cups spaghetti sauce
4 potatoes, baked and blossomed
1 cup shredded mozzarella cheese
2 tbs. grated Parmesan cheese

Heat olive oil in a large skillet over medium high heat. Add veal and quickly stir-fry until light golden brown, about 3 minutes. Remove and set aside. Add pepper to pan and cook until softened, add mushrooms and garlic and cook until tender. Season to taste. Add spaghetti sauce and bring to a simmer. Add veal and heat through. Divide mixture evenly over prepared potatoes. Top with cheeses and broil briefly to melt.

# QUICK CHILI POTATOES

Serves: 4

*This quick recipe can be frozen and reheated in the microwave.*

1 lb. ground chuck
1 cup chopped onion
2 cloves garlic, minced
1 green bell pepper, chopped
1 can (16 oz.) crushed tomatoes
   in puree
1 can (16 oz.) kidney beans,
   drained
1-2 tbs. chili powder

1 tsp. cumin
1 tsp. oregano
½ tsp. Tabasco Sauce
½ tsp. pepper
salt to taste
4 potatoes, baked and blossomed
sour cream, shredded cheddar
   or chopped onion for garnish

In a large skillet over medium high heat, cook beef with onion, garlic and green pepper until meat is no longer pink and vegetables are soft. Drain off any excess juices. Add tomatoes, beans and seasonings. Simmer for 20 minutes, adding water if mixture becomes too thick. Divide evenly over potatoes and garnish as desired.

# PORK FAJITA TOPPING

*Chicken, beef or shrimp also work well in this recipe.*

4 center-cut boneless pork
  chops
1 tsp. chili powder
1 tsp. ground cumin
1 clove garlic, minced
$1/4$ tsp. cayenne pepper
$1/2$ tsp. salt
2 tbs. salad oil
1 large green bell pepper, cut
  into strips
1 white onion, cut into quarters
4 potatoes, baked and
  blossomed
$1/2$ cup sour cream
$1/2$ cup salsa
1 avocado, diced
1 tbs. chopped cilantro
1 lime, cut into wedges

Cut pork chops into ¼-inch-thick strips. Combine chili powder, cumin, garlic, cayenne and salt in a plastic bag. Add pork and shake well to coat meat. Refrigerate several hours or overnight. Heat oil in a large skillet and sauté green pepper over very high heat until tender. Some of the pieces should be a bit charred. remove and set aside. Cut onion quarters into strips and stir-fry strips until tender. Remove and add to peppers. Turn heat to medium, adding more oil if necessary. Cook pork strips until tender and no longer pink. Add pepper and onion mixture to pan and heat through. Divide evenly over prepared potatoes and top with sour cream, salsa, diced avocado and cilantro. Serve with wedges of lime to squeeze over the top.

# PORK AND BLACK BEAN CHILI

Serves: 4

*I buy black beans at the health food store and simmer a batch for a black beans and rice salad or for this unusual chili.*

1½ lb. boneless pork loin
3 tbs. oil
1 large onion, chopped
2 cloves garlic, minced
2 tsp. ground cumin
2 tbs. chili powder
2 tsp. dried oregano

salt and pepper to taste
2 cans (16 oz. each) crushed
   tomatoes in puree
3 cups cooked black beans
4 potatoes, baked and blossomed
sour cream, shredded cheddar,
   avocado or cilantro for garnish

Chill pork until very cold. Trim off fat. Cut pork into ½-inch dice. Heat oil in a large skillet over medium heat. Add pork and cook, stirring frequently, until pork is no longer pink. Add onion and garlic; cook until onion is softened and pork is browned. Stir in remaining ingredients and simmer for 30 minutes. If mixture becomes too thick, add water. Season to taste. Divide evenly over potatoes and garnish.

# CHIMICHANGA TOPPING

Serves: 8

*This recipe is ideal for using leftovers like beef pot roast, pork, turkey or chicken. Leftover filling freezes well.*

3 cups shredded meat or poultry
1 jar (16 oz.) salsa
1 can (16 oz.) refried beans
1 can (4 oz.) diced green chiles
1 envelope taco seasoning
8 potatoes, baked and blossomed

8 oz. shredded cheddar or Monterey Jack cheese
additional salsa, sour cream, diced tomatoes, sliced green onions, sliced black olives for garnish

In a large skillet over medium heat, combine meat, salsa, beans, undrained chiles and taco seasoning. Stir gently to heat through. Divide evenly over prepared potatoes, top with cheese and garnish as desired.

# BEEF SZECHWAN

*Dark sesame oil adds a great deal of flavor to Oriental dishes. Be sure to keep it in the refrigerator so it won't turn rancid. Fresh ginger is easy to prepare using the food processor. Finely chop a large root and freeze what you don't need for later.*

1 lb. flank steak
2 tbs. low sodium soy sauce
4 tsp. sesame oil, divided
1½ tsp. sugar
1 tsp. cornstarch
2 cloves garlic, minced
1 tbs. minced ginger
¼ tsp. red pepper flakes
1 red bell pepper, cored and cut into strips

1 pkg. (8 oz.) baby corn, thawed
¼ lb. snow peas, halved on the diagonal
4 potatoes, baked and blossomed
¼ cup green onions, thinly sliced on the diagonal

Cut steak in half lengthwise. Slice across the grain into ¼-inch strips. Combine soy sauce, 2 tsp. sesame oil, sugar and cornstarch. Place meat in a plastic bag and add soy mixture, coating meat well. Refrigerate if not cooking immediately. Heat 2 tsp. sesame oil in a large skillet over medium high heat. Stir-fry aromatics — garlic, ginger and red pepper flakes — for 30 seconds. Add red bell pepper and corn and stir-fry 2 minutes. Add snow peas and cook until tender and bright green. Remove vegetables from skillet and set aside. Add beef strips to skillet and stir-fry until tender, 2 to 3 minutes. Return vegetables to skillet and heat through. Divide evenly over prepared potatoes and sprinkle with green onions.

# BEEF AND BREW SPUDS

*The flavors of this topping will remind you of merry old England. The Cordon Bleu insists you ALWAYS use dry mustard with cheese!*

1 can (12 oz.) beer
1 lb. sharp cheddar cheese, shredded
$\frac{1}{3}$ cup flour
1 tsp. Worcestershire sauce
salt to taste
cayenne to taste

$\frac{1}{2}$ tsp. dry mustard
8 oz. rare deli roast beef, cut into strips
4 potatoes, baked and blossomed
parsley sprigs for garnish

In a heavy saucepan, bring beer to a gentle boil over medium heat. In a large bowl, toss shredded cheese with flour to coat. Using a wooden spoon to stir constantly, gradually add cheese, a handful at a time, until all cheese has been added. Stir in one direction only. Add seasonings to taste. Stir in roast beef and heat through. Divide evenly over prepared potatoes and garnish with parsley.

# PORK PAPRIKASH

*When slicing meat for stir-fry dishes, always partially freeze the meat and use a very sharp knife. It will greatly speed the process.*

| | |
|---|---|
| 1 lb. boneless pork loin chops | 1/2 cup white wine |
| 1 tbs. butter | 1 cup sour cream |
| 1 tbs. oil | 1 tbs. Dijon mustard |
| salt and pepper to taste | 4 potatoes, baked and |
| 3 tsp. Hungarian paprika | blossomed |
| 2 tbs. finely chopped onion | 1 tbs. minced parsley |

Slice pork into 1/4-inch strips. Heat butter and oil in a large skillet over medium high heat. Stir-fry pork until meat is browned and cooked through. Sprinkle meat with salt and pepper, remove from skillet and set aside. Add paprika and onion to skillet and cook until onion is soft. Stir in white wine, sour cream and mustard and whisk until blended and smooth. Do not boil. Return pork to skillet and heat through. Divide evenly over potatoes. Garnish with parsley.

# REUBEN MURPHYS

Serves: 4

*Purchase corned beef at your deli to make preparation a cinch.*

1 tbs. butter
1 onion, chopped
8 oz. deli corned beef
1 can (16 oz.) sauerkraut
1 cup mayonnaise
2 tbs. chili sauce

2 tbs. dill pickles, chopped
2 tsp. lemon juice
2 tsp. sugar
4 potatoes, baked and blossomed
4 oz. Swiss cheese, shredded
2 tsp. caraway seeds, optional

Melt butter in a skillet and cook onion until soft. Cut corned beef into strips. Drain sauerkraut well and add to skillet with corned beef. Heat mixture through.

For dressing, thoroughly combine mayonnaise, chili sauce, pickles, lemon juice and sugar in a small bowl.

Divide corned beef mixture evenly over potatoes, top with dressing and sprinkle with cheese. Broil briefly to melt cheese. If desired, sprinkle with caraway seeds.

# TURKISH TOPPING

Serves: 4

*The fluffy white potato, spicy meat mixture and crisp, cool vegetables create an appealing contrast in temperature and texture.*

½ lb. ground chuck
½ lb. ground lamb
½ cup finely chopped onion
1 clove garlic, minced
½ cup ketchup
2 tbs. chopped parsley
1 tsp. dried oregano leaves
1 tsp. cinnamon

½ tsp. ground cumin
¼ tsp. cloves
1 tsp. salt
½ tsp. pepper
4 potatoes, baked and blossomed
1 green bell pepper, chopped
2 plum tomatoes, sliced
1 small red onion, cut in slivers

In a large skillet over medium high heat, cook meats, onion and garlic until onion is soft and meat is no longer pink. Drain off excess fat and add ketchup, herbs and spices. Simmer 5 minutes. Divide meat mixture evenly over potatoes and garnish with green pepper, plum tomatoes and red onion.

# GREEK TOPPING WITH CUCUMBER YOGURT SAUCE

*The meat can be marinated the day before and the sauce prepared and refrigerated. Serve with a big green salad with crumbled feta cheese and Greek olives.*

1 lb. lean boneless pork
¼ cup olive oil
¼ cup lemon juice
2 tbs. Dijon mustard
2 cloves garlic, minced
1½ tsp. crumbled oregano
1 tsp. crumbled thyme
1 tbs. olive oil

4 potatoes, baked and
   blossomed
*Cucumber Yogurt Sauce,* follows
1 tomato, seeded and diced, for
   garnish
½ small red onion, thinly
   sliced, for garnish

Trim fat from pork. Place in freezer for 30 minutes to facilitate slicing. Slice into thin bite-sized strips. Place pork in a heavy duty plastic bag. In a small bowl, combine oil, lemon juice, mustard, garlic and herbs, mixing well. Pour over pork and mix well. Refrigerate for at least 6 hours or overnight.

Drain pork and discard marinade. Heat a large skillet and add 1 tbs. oil. Stir-fry pork over medium high heat until cooked through, about 3 minutes. Divide evenly over prepared potatoes. Garnish with *Cucumber Yogurt Sauce*, tomato and onion.

## CUCUMBER YOGURT SAUCE

| | |
|---|---|
| 8 oz. plain yogurt | 1 tsp. dill |
| 1 cup diced cucumber, peeled and seeded | 1/2 tsp. seasoned salt |
| | 1 clove garlic, minced |

Combine ingredients and chill.

# ITALIAN SAUSAGE SAUTÉ

Serves: 4

*Be sure to prick the skin of the sausage in several places to allow the grease to escape and to keep sausages from bursting.*

1 lb. Italian sausages
1 cup red wine or water
2 tbs. olive oil
1 clove garlic, minced
1 large onion, thinly sliced
1 bell pepper, thinly sliced

2 cups spaghetti sauce
4 oz. mozzarella cheese, shredded
4 potatoes, baked and blossomed
2 tbs. grated Parmesan cheese

Place sausages in a large skillet and add wine or water. Simmer over medium heat for 10 minutes, turning occasionally. Remove sausages to a cutting board and cut into ½-inch slices. Wipe out skillet and add oil. Sauté garlic and onion until limp. Add sausage and bell pepper and cook until sausages are light brown and pepper is softened. Add spaghetti sauce and heat through. Divide mixture evenly over potatoes. Top with cheeses and broil briefly to melt.

# POTATOES A LA RITZ

Serves: 4

*This elegant potato dish may turn up on Lifestyles of the Rich and Famous!*

¼ cup butter
8 oz. filet mignon or other
  tender beef cut in strips
1 small onion, diced
½ cup sliced Shiitake
  mushrooms

½ cup sliced domestic
  mushrooms
½ tsp. thyme
salt and pepper to taste
1 cup sour cream
4 potatoes, baked and blossomed

Melt 2 tbs. butter in a large skillet. Quickly sauté beef over high heat until done to your liking, 1 to 2 minutes for rare. Remove from skillet and set aside. Melt remaining butter and sauté onion until soft. Add mushrooms and cook until tender. Sprinkle with seasonings. Return meat to pan and add sour cream. Heat through but do not boil. Divide evenly over prepared potatoes.

# OYSTER BEEF

Serves: 4

*For variety, add 2 cups steamed broccoli, asparagus or snow peas.*

1 lb. boneless lean beef, partially
  frozen for easy slicing
2 green onions, chopped
2 tbs. low sodium soy sauce
2 tbs. water
1 tbs. cornstarch

1 tbs. white wine
2 tbs. oil
2 tbs. oyster sauce
1 tsp. sugar
4 potatoes, baked and blossomed
toasted sesame seeds for garnish

Slice meat across the grain into $\frac{1}{4}$-inch slices. Combine green onions, soy, water, cornstarch and wine in a food processor or in a small bowl. Add meat and stir to coat well. Let stand at room temperature for 15 minutes. Heat 1 tbs. of the oil over high heat in a heavy skillet. Cook half the meat, stir-frying in a hot skillet until browned, about 2 minutes. Remove and set aside. Cook remaining meat. Return all meat to skillet. Stir in oyster sauce and sugar until combined. Divide evenly over potatoes. Sprinkle with sesame seed.

# PORK MARSALA

*This elegant entrée is easy to prepare when you use an off-the-shelf Demi Glace sauce (or prepare your own* Demi Glace, *page 9).*

| | |
|---|---|
| 1 lb. boneless pork strips | ¼ cup Marsala wine |
| ¼ cup butter, divided | 1 cup prepared *Demi Glace* |
| 1 clove garlic, minced | salt and pepper to taste |
| 1 small onion, cut in slivers | 4 potatoes, baked and |
| 1 cup mushrooms, quartered | blossomed |

Trim pork of fat and freeze for 30 minutes to facilitate slicing. Cut into bite-sized strips. In a large skillet over medium-high heat, melt 2 tbs. of the butter. Stir-fry pork until cooked through, about 3 to 4 minutes, remove and set aside. Melt remaining butter in skillet and cook garlic until tender. Add onion and sauté until limp. Add mushrooms and cook until tender. Pour wine into pan and bring to a boil. Stir in *Demi Glace*. Taste and adjust seasoning. Divide evenly over potatoes.

# PRIME RIB POTATOES

Serves: 4

*Next time you go out for prime rib, order the biggest cut available and take the leftovers home in a doggie bag. This makes a sensational dinner the next day.*

1 cup sour cream
1 tbs. horseradish
2 tsp. Dijon mustard
1 tsp. salt
1 lb. prime rib, cut in strips

1 cup beef broth
4 potatoes, baked and
  blossomed
1 cup shredded cheddar cheese
2 green onions, thinly sliced

Combine sour cream, horseradish, mustard and salt in a small bowl. Heat meat strips in beef broth until warmed through. Divide sour cream mixture evenly over prepared potatoes, top with meat, sprinkle with cheese and top with green onions.

# VEAL PICCATA

*This is a classic Italian preparation with lemon juice and parsley.*

3 tbs. flour
salt and pepper to taste
1 lb. veal scaloppine
2 tbs. olive oil
2 tbs. butter
1 clove garlic, minced

1 cup chicken stock
juice and zest of 1 lemon
1 tbs. capers
4 potatoes, baked and
   blossomed
2 tbs. minced parsley

Place flour, salt and pepper in a plastic bag. Cut veal into strips. Dredge in a bag and shake off excess. In a skillet over medium high heat, melt oil and butter. Sauté veal until browned on both sides. Remove and set aside. In skillet drippings, cook garlic until soft, about 1 minute. Add chicken stock and cook until thickened, about 4 minutes. Add lemon zest, juice and capers. Return veal to pan and heat through. Divide evenly over prepared potatoes. Sprinkle with parsley.

# CHICKEN AND SAUSAGE

Serves: 4

*Serve with a big green salad with red and green peppers and a tangy vinaigrette. To seed a tomato, cut in half horizontally and squeeze each half, cut side down, over the sink.*

2 tbs. butter
1 whole chicken breast, skinned, boned and cut into 1-inch cubes
1 clove garlic, minced
salt and pepper to taste
1/4 lb. mushrooms
1/2 lb. Italian link sausage, cut into 1-inch slices
1 cup white wine
1 tomato, seeded and diced
1/2 tsp. red pepper flakes
4 potatoes, baked and blossomed
1/2 cup grated Parmesan cheese

Heat butter in a skillet over medium heat, add chicken and garlic and stir fry until chicken is cooked through. Sprinkle with salt and pepper. Remove and set aside. Add mushrooms to skillet and cook until tender. Remove and set aside. Add sausage and cover with white wine. Boil gently until sausage is done. Return chicken and mushrooms to skillet, add tomato and red pepper flakes and heat through. Divide evenly over prepared potatoes and sprinkle with Parmesan.

# CHICKEN AND CREAM CHEESE

Serves: 4

*Rich and delicious! Garnish with sliced green onions, black olives, salsa and cilantro for real south-of-the-border flair.*

2 tbs. butter
1 large onion, sliced
2 cups diced cooked chicken
8 oz. cream cheese, room temperature
1 can (4 oz.) chopped green chiles
1/4 cup chopped pimiento
1/2 cup milk
salt and pepper to taste
4 potatoes, baked and blossomed
1 cup shredded cheddar cheese
sliced green onions, black olives, salsa or other garnish

Heat butter in a large skillet and cook onion until golden. Add chicken and cream cheese, cut into cubes. Stir gently until cream cheese begins to melt. Add chiles and pimiento and thin with milk as needed. Season to taste and divide evenly over prepared potatoes. Sprinkle with cheddar and garnish with suggested condiments.

# KENTUCKY HOT BROWN

*This is a variation of a dish from a hotel in Louisville, Kentucky.*

12 slices cooked, crumbled
   bacon, drippings reserved
2 tbs. minced shallots or onion
3 tbs. flour
1 1/4 cups milk
1 tsp. Worcestershire sauce
1/8 tsp. cayenne pepper

1/8 tsp. dry mustard
1 tbs. sherry
4 oz. sharp cheddar, shredded
2–3 cups diced cooked chicken
4 potatoes, baked and blossomed
4 tbs. grated Parmesan cheese

In bacon drippings, sauté shallots until soft. Whisk in flour and cook over medium heat until thickened. Add milk and continue to whisk until bubbly. Add Worcestershire, cayenne, mustard and sherry. Add cheese, stirring continuously. (Tip: for smoother sauces, stir in one direction only.) Add chicken to sauce and heat through. Divide sauce evenly over potatoes and sprinkle with crumbled bacon and Parmesan. Set briefly under broiler until bubbly.

# CHICKEN LIVERS IN CREAM

Serves: 4

*If you love chicken livers, this dish is for you.*

1/4 cup butter
1 lb. chicken livers
1 tbs. minced shallots
2 tbs. cognac
1 cup heavy cream
salt and pepper to taste
4 potatoes, baked and blossomed
2 tbs. finely chopped parsley

Rinse chicken livers and pat dry with paper towels. Cut each liver in half. In a large skillet over medium heat, melt butter and sauté livers and shallots. Push mixture to side of pan and add cognac. Ignite. Allow flames to subside. Stir in cream and season to taste with salt and pepper. Divide evenly over prepared potatoes and sprinkle with parsley.

# CHILI BLANCO

Serves: 4

*This chili is "New Wave" as it uses ground turkey and pink beans instead of the more traditional ingredients.*

2 tbs. oil
1 lb. ground turkey
1 large onion, chopped
2 cloves garlic, minced
2 tbs. chili powder
2 tsp. cumin
1 tsp. dried oregano
salt and pepper to taste
1 can (16 oz.) chicken broth

1 can (4 oz.) can chopped green chiles
1 can (16 oz.) crushed tomatoes in puree
1 can (16 oz.) pink kidney beans
4 potatoes, baked and blossomed
sour cream, avocado, salsa, cilantro or other garnish

Heat oil in a large skillet over medium high heat. Cook turkey, onion and garlic until turkey is light brown and onion is soft. Drain off excess fat or juices. Add remaining ingredients and simmer 30 minutes. Season to taste. Divide evenly over potatoes and garnish.

# CABO SAN LUCAS

Serves: 4

*This flavorful topping reminds me of the sunny flavors of Mexico.*

1 cup sour cream
1/2 cup salsa
2 tbs. oil
1 clove garlic, minced
2 whole chicken breasts,
  skinned, boned and diced
4 potatoes, baked and
  blossomed

1 cup shredded jalapeño cheese
1 avocado, peeled, pitted and
  diced
1 tomato, seeded and diced
1/2 cup chopped red onion
1 tbs. chopped cilantro,
  optional

Combine sour cream and salsa in a small bowl. Heat oil and sauté garlic until soft. Add chicken and stir-fry until cooked through. Divide evenly over prepared potatoes and top with sour cream sauce. Sprinkle with cheese and top with avocado, tomato, red onion and cilantro.

# CHICKEN ROMA

Serves: 4

*We use freshly shredded Parmesan, rather than grated Parmesan, in salads and as a topping. It adds more freshness, flavor and visual appeal to the finished dish.*

2 chicken breasts, skinned, boned and cubed
1 clove garlic, minced
1 cup mushrooms, sliced
1 small onion, diced
1 small jar marinated artichoke hearts, drained, marinade reserved
1 cup tomato or spaghetti sauce
4 potatoes, baked and blossomed
¼ cup shredded Parmesan cheese

Pour artichoke marinade into a skillet and sauté chicken over medium heat until cooked through. Remove and set aside. Sauté garlic and onion until soft. Add mushrooms and cook until limp. Coarsely chop artichoke hearts. Stir into mixture together with tomato sauce and heat through. Divide evenly over prepared potatoes and sprinkle with Parmesan.

# CHICKEN TERIYAKI

*For an unusual garnish, place four green onions in the microwave and cook on high for 60 seconds. Cool under cold water and tie each onion into a knot. Trim ends evenly with scissors.*

$1/2$ cup soy sauce
$1/2$ cup dark brown sugar
1 clove garlic, minced
2 tbs. freshly grated ginger
4 chicken thighs, skinned, boned and cubed
2 tbs. oil
$1/4$ lb. snow peas
4 potatoes, baked and blossomed
$1/4$ cup sliced green onions
$1/2$ cup chopped cashews

Combine soy, sugar, garlic and ginger in a small bowl. Pour over chicken in a plastic zip lock bag. Refrigerate for several hours or overnight. Heat 2 tbs. oil in a skillet over medium high heat. Drain chicken and stir-fry until chicken is almost done. Add snow peas and cook until tender-crisp and bright green. If mixture becomes too dry, add marinade to pan. Divide mixture evenly over potatoes and sprinkle with green onions and cashews.

# JERKED CHICKEN

*This is Caribbean in origin. You can use pork as well as chicken. Be sure to wear plastic gloves when handling the jalapeño and be careful of your eyes.*

4 sweet potatoes or yams, baked and blossomed
2 chicken breasts, skinned, boned and cubed

## MARINADE

1/2 cup sliced green onion
1 fresh jalapeño chile, finely
  diced
1 tbs. soy sauce
1 tbs. lime juice
1 tsp. ground allspice

1/2 tsp. dry mustard
1/2 bay leaf, finely crumbled
1 clove garlic, minced
1 tsp. salt
1/2 tsp. thyme
1/4 tsp. cinnamon

Combine marinade ingredients and pour over prepared chicken in a plastic bag. Refrigerate for several hours or overnight.

Chicken mixture may be stir-fried or grilled but grilling is more authentic. To stir-fry, heat 2 tbs. oil in a skillet over medium heat, add chicken and cook 3 to 4 minutes or until cooked through. To grill, soak wooden skewers in water for 1 hour. Thread chicken onto skewers and grill, turning once, until chicken is cooked through. Divide mixture evenly over prepared potatoes.

## PINEAPPLE SALSA

Makes 1 1/4 cups

*Serve with Jerked Chicken.*

1 can (8 oz.) crushed pineapple in juice
1/4 cup chopped red onion
1 jalapeño chile, minced

1/4 cup chopped fresh cilantro
2 tsp. lime juice
1 tsp. red wine vinegar
1/4 tsp. salt

Combine all ingredients and chill.

# CHICKEN VEGETABLE TOPPING

Serves: 4

*With the variety of spaghetti sauces now available at the grocery store, it's easy to put together a healthy and delicious potato topping in just minutes. Use any fresh vegetables you might have on hand: carrots, peas, onions, mushrooms, green beans or celery.*

2 tbs. butter
1 yellow summer squash, sliced
   into ½-inch rounds
4 green onions, sliced
1 lb. ground chicken

2 cups spaghetti sauce
salt and pepper to taste
4 potatoes, baked and blossomed
½ cup shredded Parmesan
   cheese

Melt butter and sauté squash in a large skillet over medium high heat until beginning to soften. Add green onions and cook mixture until onion is limp. Remove and set aside. In the same skillet, sauté chicken until it is cooked through. Drain off any juices. Add vegetable mixture and spaghetti sauce. Simmer 10 minutes. Season to taste. Divide evenly over potatoes. Sprinkle with Parmesan.

# CHICKEN WITH HERBS

Serves: 4

*If you grow your own herbs, this is a great way to add freshness and wonderful flavor, plus it is low in calories.*

2 tbs. butter
2 chicken breasts, skinned,
   boned and cubed
1 clove garlic, minced
10 sprigs parsley, chopped
10 basil leaves, chopped

2 tsp. fresh tarragon, chopped
1 cup chicken broth
1 tbs. Dijon mustard
salt and pepper to taste
4 potatoes, baked and blossomed

Heat butter in a large skillet and stir-fry chicken with garlic until chicken is done. Add herbs and chicken broth. Whisk in mustard and season to taste with salt and pepper. Divide evenly over prepared potatoes.

# CHICKEN ORIENTAL

Serves: 4

*Needless to say, this is also good on rice.*

1 lb. ground chicken
2 tbs. oil
1 onion, chopped
2 carrots, chopped
2 stalks celery, chopped
1½ cups prepared teriyaki sauce
salt and pepper to taste
4 potatoes, baked and blossomed

In a skillet over medium high heat, cook chicken until crumbly. Remove and set aside. Wipe out pan with paper toweling. Heat oil and sauté onion until soft. Add carrots and celery and cook until tender-crisp. Return chicken to the pan and add teriyaki sauce. Heat through. Taste and correct seasoning. Divide evenly over potatoes.

# CHICKEN AND ZUCCHINI

*Boneless cuts of chicken make great timesavers in the kitchen!*

2 tbs. oil
2 tbs. butter
12 oz. chicken, cut into strips
1 large onion, cut into slivers
2 cloves garlic, minced
2 small zucchini, sliced

1 cup heavy cream
1 cup shredded Parmesan cheese
salt and pepper to taste
1 tsp. freshly grated nutmeg
4 potatoes, baked and blossomed

Heat oil and butter in a large pan over medium high heat. Sauté chicken until cooked through and beginning to brown. Remove and set aside. Add onion and garlic to pan and cook until soft. Add zucchini and cook until zucchini and onion begin to brown. Pour in cream. Return chicken to pan and sprinkle with half of the Parmesan. Cook, stirring constantly, until mixture begins to thicken. Season to taste with salt and pepper. Add nutmeg. Divide evenly into potatoes and sprinkle with remaining Parmesan.

# CHICKEN JERUSALEM

*For a variation, substitute ¼ cup sun-dried tomatoes for fresh tomato.*

¼ cup butter, divided
2 chicken breasts, skinned,
  boned and cubed
1 small onion, cut in slivers
1 cup sliced mushrooms
1 tomato, seeded and diced

1 cup artichoke quarters
¼ cup sliced black olives
¼ cup brandy
¾ cup heavy cream
¼ cup grated Parmesan cheese
4 potatoes, baked and blossomed

Melt 2 tbs. butter in a large skillet over medium high heat. Sauté chicken breasts until cooked through, stirring frequently. Remove and set aside. Melt remaining butter and cook onion until limp. Add mushrooms and sauté until tender. Add tomato, artichoke, olives and chicken to skillet and heat through. In a small saucepan, heat brandy and ignite. Carefully pour into skillet. Stir until flames die down. Add cream and bring to a boil. Stir in cheese until melted. Divide evenly over prepared potatoes.

# CHICKEN TETRAZZINI

Serves: 4

*This mixture is traditionally served over spaghetti but it is rich, delicious and comforting served over a fluffy baked potato.*

3 tbs. butter
3 tbs. flour
1 cup chicken broth
½ cup cream
salt and white pepper to taste
2 cups diced cooked chicken,
   preferably white meat

¼ cup sliced mushrooms
¼ cup dry sherry
pinch of freshly grated nutmeg
4 potatoes, baked and
   blossomed
¼ cup grated Parmesan cheese

Melt butter in a medium saucepan, whisk in flour and cook for 2 minutes, stirring constantly. Add chicken broth and cream and bring to a boil. Add salt and pepper, chicken, mushrooms, sherry and nutmeg. Simmer 5 minutes. Taste and correct seasoning. Divide evenly over prepared potatoes and sprinkle with Parmesan.

# BISTRO CHICKEN

*Roasted red peppers add so much flavor to appetizers and main dishes—and opening a jar is quicker than roasting them yourself.*

2 whole chicken breasts, skinned and boned
2 tbs. oil
3 cloves garlic, minced
1 large onion, cut into slivers

$\frac{1}{2}$ cup roasted red pepper, sliced
1 cup sour cream
salt and pepper to taste
4 potatoes, baked and blossomed
2 oz. prosciutto ham, cut in strips

Cut chicken breasts into $\frac{1}{2}$-inch strips. In a large skillet over medium-high heat, cook chicken strips in oil until opaque. Remove and set aside. Add garlic and onion slivers and cook until golden brown. Stir in roasted peppers and sour cream. Return chicken to skillet and heat through. Season to taste with salt and pepper. Do not boil. Divide chicken mixture evenly over potatoes. Garnish with prosciutto.

# GREEK TAVERNA TOPPING

Serves: 4

*Cinnamon, allspice and tomato give this topping an unusual Greek flavor. Use leftover dark turkey meat or ground turkey.*

2 tbs. olive oil
1 small onion, chopped
1 clove garlic, minced
1 small carrot, finely diced
2 cups shredded dark turkey
  meat or cooked ground turkey
1 cup tomato sauce
½ cup robust red wine

1 bay leaf
1 tsp. cinnamon
¼ tsp. ground allspice
¼ tsp. red pepper flakes
½ tsp. ground black pepper
4 potatoes, baked and
  blossomed

In a heavy skillet, heat olive oil. Sauté onion until soft. Add garlic and carrot and cook for 3 minutes, stirring over medium high heat. Add remaining ingredients and simmer for 30 minutes. Remove bay leaf and divide evenly over prepared potatoes.

# HOT AND SOUR SHRIMP

*This quick stir-fry is low in calories. Vary it with shiitake mushrooms.*

2 tbs. low sodium soy sauce
2 tbs. rice vinegar
1 tsp. sugar
$1/4-1/2$ tsp. red pepper flakes
2 cloves garlic, minced
1 tsp. dark sesame oil
1 lb. medium shrimp, peeled

1 tbs. oil
4 green onions, sliced on the
  diagonal into 2-inch lengths
8 oz. fresh mushrooms, sliced
2 cups snow peas, trimmed and
  sliced in half diagonally
4 potatoes, baked and blossomed

Combine soy, vinegar, sugar, red pepper flakes, garlic and sesame oil. Marinate shrimp in mixture for several hours or overnight. Heat oil in a large skillet over medium high heat. Sauté green onions for 1 minute; add mushrooms and cook for 2 minutes longer. Add snow peas and cook for 1 minute. Pour shrimp and marinade into skillet and stir-fry for 2 minutes or until shrimp turns pink. Divide evenly over prepared potatoes.

# PAELLA POTATOES

*All the ingredients in the Spanish dish, paella, served on a potato.*

4 tbs. olive oil, divided
2 cloves garlic, minced
1 onion, chopped
1 tsp. turmeric
1 boneless chicken breast, cubed
4 oz. Italian sausage links, cut in
  1/2-inch slices

1/2 green bell pepper, diced
1 tomato, seeded and diced
1/2 cup frozen green peas
4 oz. medium shrimp with tails
salt and pepper to taste
4 potatoes, baked and blossomed

Heat 2 tbs. of olive oil in a large skillet over medium high heat. Add garlic and onion and sauté until softened. Sprinkle with turmeric. Remove and set aside. Add chicken to skillet and cook until opaque. Remove and set aside. Add sausage and cook through. Drain off fat. Add green pepper and tomato and cook until heated through. Return onion mixture and chicken to skillet. Add peas and shrimp. Cook until shrimp are done. Season and divide evenly over potatoes.

# SCAMPI MARNIER

*Scampi refers to the tail portion of different kinds of small lobster, also known as the Dublin Bay prawn, but Scampi is also used in the U.S to refer to large shrimp, cooked in garlic butter.*

1/4 cup butter
2 cloves garlic, minced
1 lb. fresh scampi
2 tbs. white wine
1 cup prepared pesto
1 cup prepared spaghetti sauce
4 potatoes, baked and blossomed
1/4 cup finely minced fresh parsley

Heat butter in a large skillet over medium high heat. Add garlic and sauté until soft. Add scampi and quickly stir-fry until almost opaque. Add wine, pesto and spaghetti sauce and heat through. Divide evenly over prepared potatoes and sprinkle with parsley.

# SHRIMP MILANESE

*Use fresh basil, if you can. Thinly snip the leaves into strips with scissors. This is called a "chiffonade".*

| | |
|---|---|
| 2 tbs. olive oil | 1 cup tomato or spaghetti sauce |
| 1 clove garlic, minced | 1 cup cooked baby shrimp |
| 1 cup sliced mushrooms | 4 potatoes, baked and |
| 2 tomatoes, seeded and | blossomed |
| chopped | fresh basil strips |
| ¼ cup sliced green onion | ¼ cup freshly shredded |
| ¼ cup sliced black olives | Parmesan cheese |

In a skillet, heat oil and sauté garlic over medium high heat until soft. Add mushrooms and cook until tender. Stir in tomatoes and green onion and cook until limp. Add olives, sauce and shrimp and heat through. Divide evenly over prepared potatoes and garnish with basil and Parmesan.

# SCALLOPS BEARNAISE

*Bearnaise is a classic French sauce made of egg yolks and clarified butter, with tarragon vinegar and shallots. Knorr Swiss makes an excellent prepared Bearnaise. Asparagus makes a nice side dish with this recipe.*

2 strips bacon, diced
2 green onions, sliced
1 cup sliced mushrooms
8 oz. scallops
2 tbs. white wine

1 pkg. Bearnaise sauce mix,
   prepared per instructions
4 potatoes, baked and
   blossomed

In a large skillet, sauté bacon until limp. Add green onions and mushrooms and cook until mushrooms are tender. Add scallops and wine and cook until scallops are opaque. Stir in Bearnaise and heat through. Do not boil or mixture will curdle. Divide evenly over prepared potatoes.

# CIOPINNO POTATOES

*A crisp green salad, a glass of wine and you're all set for a feast.*

1 onion, chopped
1 clove garlic, minced
2 tbs. olive oil
1 cup chopped tomatoes in
  puree
¼ cup white wine
1 tbs. tomato paste
1 tsp. basil

1 tsp. oregano
1 cup crab meat
1 cup cooked baby shrimp
hot pepper sauce and black
  pepper to taste
4 large potatoes, baked and
  blossomed

In a medium skillet, sauté onion and garlic in olive oil until softened. Add tomatoes, wine, tomato paste and seasonings. Simmer 15 minutes. Stir in crab meat and shrimp and heat through. Taste and add pepper sauce and black pepper. Divide evenly over prepared potatoes.

# CRAB MORNAY

Serves: 4

*In the Pacific Northwest, we are lucky to get fresh Dungeness crab. It's expensive but worth every penny. Mornay refers to the French sauce, similar to Bechamel, with shredded cheese added.*

¼ cup butter
4 green onions, finely chopped
¼ cup minced parsley
1 tbs. flour
1 cup cream
1 cup shredded Swiss cheese

1 tbs. sherry
salt and cayenne to taste
12 oz. fresh crab meat
4 potatoes, baked and
   blossomed

In a saucepan over medium heat, melt butter and sauté onions and parsley until soft. Sprinkle with flour and stir to combine. Add cream and stir until smooth. Slowly add cheese, and stir until melted. Season to taste with sherry, salt and cayenne. Add crab and heat through. Divide evenly over prepared potatoes.

# SMOKED SALMON BRUNCH

*This makes a nice lunch or brunch if you use the optional scrambled eggs. Be sure to use only the finest cold smoked salmon or lox. Although it's expensive, a little goes a long way.*

1/4 cup butter
1/2 cup thinly sliced green onions
16 slices smoked salmon
salt and pepper to taste
4 potatoes, baked and blossomed
4 eggs, lightly scrambled, optional
1 cup shredded Swiss cheese

Heat butter in a small skillet until foamy. Cook green onions over medium heat until limp. Cut salmon into 1/2-inch strips. Add to pan and cook until heated through. Season to taste. Divide evenly into prepared potatoes and top with scrambled eggs, if desired. Sprinkle evenly with cheese.

# LOBSTER AND SHRIMP

*Meat from one lobster tail is enough for four servings.*

3 tbs. butter
2 tbs. sliced almonds
½ cup sour cream
¼ cup dry vermouth
1 tsp. salt
1 cup sliced cooked lobster (meat from 1 tail)
½ cup cooked baby shrimp
4 potatoes, baked and blossomed

In a medium skillet, melt butter and sauté almonds over medium heat until golden. Remove and set aside. In a small bowl, combine sour cream, vermouth and salt. Add lobster and shrimp to the skillet and stir until heated through. Add sour cream mixture and combine. Divide evenly over prepared potatoes and sprinkle with reserved almonds.

# TASTE OF ITALY TOPPING

Serves: 4

*This version is vegetarian, but cooked Italian sausage, slivers of salami, pepperoni or other Italian meats would be nice additions.*

1 jar (6 oz.) marinated artichoke hearts, drained, juice reserved
1 clove garlic, minced
3 Italian plum tomatoes, coarsely chopped
¼ cup sliced ripe olives
1 tbs. chopped fresh parsley
1 tsp. crumbled oregano
4 potatoes, baked and blossomed
1 cup shredded provolone cheese

Pour marinade into a skillet and sauté garlic over medium high heat until soft. Add artichokes, tomatoes and olives and heat through. Sprinkle with herbs. Divide evenly into prepared potatoes and sprinkle with cheese.

# POTATOES PRIMAVERA

Serves: 4

*Pass around extra shredded Parmesan to go on top.*

1 cup small broccoli florets
1 cup thinly sliced carrots
1 cup fresh green beans, sliced
1 small zucchini, cut in slivers
1 red bell pepper, cut into strips
8 oz. medium-size shrimp,
peeled and deveined
³/₄ cup heavy cream
¹/₂ cup chicken broth
¹/₄ cup grated Parmesan cheese
4 potatoes, baked and blossomed
freshly ground black pepper

Bring a large pot of water to a boil. Add broccoli, carrots and green beans; cook 4 minutes. Add zucchini and bell pepper and cook 2 minutes longer. Add shrimp and cook until opaque. Pour into a strainer and refresh with cold water to stop cooking process.

Combine cream, broth and cheese in a small saucepan and cook over medium heat, stirring constantly, until slightly thickened. Add vegetables and shrimp and heat through. Taste and adjust seasoning. Pour over potatoes. Sprinkle with freshly ground black pepper.

# VEGETABLE SAUTÉ WITH PESTO

*You can use any fresh vegetables you have on hand.*

2 tbs. oil
1 clove garlic, minced
2 carrots, thinly sliced
2 stalks celery, thinly sliced
1 onion, chopped
1 red bell pepper, sliced
1 zucchini, sliced

8 oz. fresh mushrooms, sliced
1/2 cup prepared pesto
4 potatoes, baked and
    blossomed
1/2 cup shredded Parmesan
    cheese

Heat oil in a large skillet over medium high heat. Stir-fry garlic, carrots, celery and onion until soft. Add pepper, zucchini and mushrooms and cook until beginning to brown. Stir in pesto. Divide evenly over prepared potatoes and sprinkle with Parmesan.

# ZUCCHINI AND CHILE TOPPING

*This is a great recipe to use up those zucchini from your fridge.*

1 tbs. oil
1 tbs. butter
1 onion, thinly sliced
2 zucchini, sliced ½-inch thick
   on the diagonal
2 tomatoes, seeded and
   chopped

1 can (4 oz.) diced green chiles
salt and pepper to taste
1 cup sour cream
4 potatoes, baked and blossomed
1 cup shredded Monterey Jack
   cheese

In a large skillet over medium high heat, combine oil and butter and sauté onion until soft. Add zucchini and cook until beginning to brown. Add tomatoes and chiles and heat through. Sprinkle with salt and pepper. Stir in sour cream and heat through, but do not boil. Divide evenly over prepared potatoes and sprinkle with cheese. Broil briefly to melt cheese.

# VEGGIE POTATO

*This is a great way to use leftover vegetables and cheeses. Whenever I'm down to the last chunk of cheese, I shred it and put it in a zip lock bag in the freezer. I have quite an assortment of cheeses — Swiss, cheddar, Monterey Jack, havarti — all shredded and ready to go for topping potatoes, pizzas or sandwiches.*

1 small onion, chopped
2 tbs. butter
2 cups cooked broccoli florets
1 cup cooked cauliflower florets
1 cup cooked carrot sliced

½ cup ranch dressing
4 potatoes, baked and blossomed
1 cup shredded cheese
¼ cup cooked, crumbled
    bacon, optional

In a medium skillet, sauté onion in butter until limp. Add vegetables and heat through. Divide evenly over prepared potatoes. Drizzle each with 2 tbs. ranch dressing. Sprinkle with cheese and top with bacon, if desired.

# VEGETABLE MELANGE WITH BALSAMIC VINEGAR

*Balsamic vinegar adds wonderful flavor to so many foods. This makes a light and healthy entrée that's low in fat and high in flavor.*

3 tbs. olive oil

2 cloves garlic, minced

1 large onion, chopped

2 small zucchini, sliced into
 $\frac{1}{2}$-inch rounds

1 cup mushrooms, sliced

$\frac{1}{4}$ cup balsamic vinegar

1 to 2 tsp. sugar

4 potatoes, baked and
 blossomed

salt and pepper

Heat oil in a skillet over medium high heat. Sauté garlic and onion until soft. Add zucchini and cook until browned on the edges. Add mushrooms and continue cooking until they are soft. Drizzle with vinegar, taste and add sugar to your liking. Divide evenly over prepared potatoes. Sprinkle with salt and pepper to taste.

# ARTICHOKES WITH CHAMPAGNE TOPPING

Serves: 4

*This is an elegant side dish to serve with filet mignon or all by itself for a meal. Be sure to have a glass of champagne while you're fixing the sauce!*

4 oz. bacon, diced
1 onion, chopped
1 tbs. chopped shallot
½ cup chopped bell pepper
4 oz. mushrooms, sliced
1 pkg. (10 oz.) frozen
  artichokes, thawed

1 cup *Demi Glace*, page 9
¼ cup champagne
1 tsp. Worcestershire sauce
4 potatoes, baked and blossomed
1 tbs. finely minced parsley

In a large skillet, sauté bacon until it begins to brown. Add onion, shallot and green pepper and cook until softened. Stir in mushrooms and cook until tender. Add artichokes, *Demi Glace*, champagne and Worcestershire. Heat through. Divide evenly over prepared potatoes. Garnish with parsley.

# POSH POTATOES

*Leeks have a nice mellow flavor — a nice change of pace in this unusual topping.*

1 leek
¼ cup butter
1 cup sliced mushrooms
1 tsp. tarragon
2 tbs. flour
1 tbs. white wine

1 cup chicken broth
1 cup diced Brie cheese, rind
  removed
salt and white pepper to taste
4 potatoes, baked and blossomed

Prepare leek by washing thoroughly. Trim off root ends and most of the green leaves. Cut leek into ½-inch rounds. Blanch, steam or microwave until tender. In a large skillet over medium high heat, melt butter. Sauté mushrooms until tender. Add prepared leek to skillet. Sprinkle with tarragon and flour. Stir in white wine and broth and bring to a gentle boil. Slowly stir in cheese until melted. Season to taste. Divide evenly over prepared potatoes.

# INDEX